THE OFFICIAL WORKBOOK TO
FINDING YOUR
YOUR

WHEN YOU'RE READY FOR
THE LIFE YOU REALLY WANT

CINDY CARRILLO

Nxt
PUBLISHING
RIDGWAY, COLORADO

Published by
Nxt Publishing
CC Blue Enterprises LTD
244 Peaceful Way
Ridgway, CO 81432

Manuscript created in collaboration with Rick Killian,
Killian Creative, Boulder, Colorado. www.killiancreative.com

Design by Peter Gloege | LOOK Design Studio

Library of Congress Control Number: 2024915608

Paperback ISBN: 979-8-9887023-2-0

Printed in the United States of America

24 25 26 27 28 29 30 31 32 33 (IS) 10 9 8 7 6 5 4 3 2 1

TABLE OF CONTENTS

Welcome to the Finding Your Nxt Workbook!

As readers of *Finding Your Nxt*, I wanted to provide you with a place to personally process the steps and action items necessary for moving from one place in life to another. It's one thing to read *my* story and learn about the steps I took as I went through the process of finding my Nxt . . . but it's another to initiate and process change on your own, for *your own life*. And sometimes it's nice to have a dedicated space to do just that.

The set-up of the Workbook follows the chapters of the book and includes the following:

- ✧ A short summary of the story

- ✧ A summary of the lessons presented in the book to help you connect the dots

- ✧ Questions to help you reflect on those lessons and dig deeper into your own rationale and process for moving forward in your life.

- ✧ And finally, each chapter ends with space for you to write notes, thoughts, and personal musings about situations in your life that apply to each lesson you might be facing.

The Workbook can be helpful while you are reading the book, allowing you to process your own thoughts as you reflect on my experiences of growth and development, or use it as a guide to work through the lessons outlined in the book, applying them to your own personal situation.

This isn't a Workbook I expect anyone to "finish" in one sitting or apply to only *one* Nxt step or phase of your life. Instead, I hope you use it as a tool over time whenever you process a change, especially during those moments when you really need to be intentional about which direction you want your life to move.

I hope it's useful for you.

Warmly,
Cindy

1

Initiate a Change

CHAPTER 1

Initiate a Change

For more than twenty years, I built and ran my company and loved every single thing about it with every part of my being. We were kicking ass on all fronts! But none of that was the issue. The problem was that my vision for growing the company into the future was starting to dim. My inability to see how to move the business forward into its Nxt stage of development was a clear signal—to me, at least—that I was no longer the right person to be in charge. So I had to initiate a change.

Lessons Learned

1. You Get to Initiate a Change

If you think about it, I bet every important change you've ever made in your life began when you chose to initiate it. It's like facing a closed door in front of you and deciding it's the right time to open it. It's the way change begins. I believe that good stuff happens when you initiate changes in your life!

When was the last time you initiated a change in your life? Describe the situation:

_____

_____

_____

_____

_____

_____

_____

_____

_____

_____

What prompted you to initiate that change? How did you know it was time?

_____

_____

_____

_____

_____

_____

_____

_____

_____

_____

When was the last time you initiated a change in your life? Describe the situation:

1._____

_____

2._____

_____

3._____

_____

4._____

_____

5._____

_____

6._____

_____

2. The Three Areas of Change

To find your Nxt, you must first decide to initiate a change from what you are currently doing, to something else in one, two, or all three areas of your life, including:

A. Your Work   B. Your Primary Relationship   C. Your Lifestyle

Describe a situation in which you initiated a change in each of the 3 areas of change.
A. Your Work:

_____

_____

_____

_____

_____

_____

_____

B. Your Primary Relationship:

_____

_____

_____

_____

_____

_____

_____

C. Your Lifestyle:

_____

_____

_____

_____

_____

_____

_____

Which of the three areas was the most difficult for you to initiate a change? Why?

_____

_____

_____

_____

_____

_____

_____

3. The Ripple Effects of Change

It's difficult to initiate a change in your work, your relationship, or your lifestyle and not have it also affect the other two. Big changes tend to reverberate without boundaries.

Can you think about a time when a change in one area of your life ended up affecting a change in one or both of the other areas? Describe what happened.

_____

_____

_____

_____

_____

_____

_____

_____

_____

_____

_____

_____

_____

4. The Context of Change

It's Important to Provide Context to Others who Might Be Affected by Changes You Initiate.

We know that changes don't happen in a vacuum. And we know that change is uncomfortable for most people. So it's incredibly important to anticipate the discomfort and be prepared to provide context to those you know will be affected by a change you initiate.

Describe a situation in your work life when providing context to others would be especially important.

_____

_____

_____

_____

_____

_____

_____

_____

Describe a situation when initiating a change in your lifestyle would have ramifications to others in your work or personal life.

_____

_____

_____

_____

_____

_____

_____

_____

_____

What are the benefits of providing the context of a change to others you work with? Define 3-6 benefits.

1. _____
_____

2. _____
_____

3. _____
_____

4. _____
_____

5. _____
_____

6. _____
_____

What are the benefits of providing the context of a change to your primary person? Define 3-6 benefits.

1. _____
_____

2. _____
_____

3. _____
_____

4. _____
_____

5. _____
_____

6. _____
_____

What are the benefits of providing the context of a change you want to make in your lifestyle to important people in your life?

Define 3-6 benefits.

1. _____

   _____

2. _____

   _____

3. _____

   _____

4. _____

   _____

5. _____

   _____

6. _____

   _____

Notes, Thoughts, and Personal Musings

2

Follow Your Dreams

CHAPTER 2

Follow Your Dreams

In the months leading up to the final closing on the sale of my company, I didn't have any idea what I was going to do, so I'd just tell people I was going to "retire." At 53, I was far too young (in my opinion) to be retired, but since I had no intention of starting another company or getting a *real* job, it became an easy response.

As the reality of the sale was beginning to sink in, however, and people really wanted to know what my future plans were, I began embellishing my thoughts about what was Nxt. I would close my eyes and say (with a bit of dramatic flair), "I think I want to find a beautiful piece of land in the mountains where I can spend my remaining days looking out at a gorgeous view of snow-packed peaks (my hand sweeping across the sky) while sitting in a comfortable rocking chair on a covered deck, wearing a really big hat." That turned out to be the big dream I was meant to follow.

Lessons Learned

1. You Get More Than One Dream

How many times have you been told you should have *one* purpose in life? Or you should find one big passion to work on your entire life? Or one big audacious lifelong dream to work toward? For your *whole* life?

What if instead of trying to create one big dream to drive you forward, you allowed yourself to have a bunch of dreams along the way?

The difference between what you might have been taught about having one big audacious dream and the process of finding your Nxt is that each stage of your life can have its own dream, and its own Nxt.

Do you allow yourself to dream? If so, how and when? If not, why not?

_____

_____

_____

_____

_____

_____

_____

Describe a dream (small or large) that you have been putting off.

_____

_____

_____

_____

_____

_____

_____

_____

What are the circumstances that have caused you to put it off?

_____

_____

_____

_____

_____

_____

What circumstances, or perspective, is making you delay starting to live your dream today? What would it take to change those?

_____

_____

_____

_____

_____

_____

If you had all of the time and resources available, what dream would you want to be living now?

_____

_____

_____

_____

_____

2. How Do You Know Which Dream to Follow?

It's best to be picky and develop a level of rigor when deciding which Nxt dream you want to spend your time and energy moving toward. Your Nxt dream should not be a frivolous idea that you throw out into the universe without any intention of acting on. Secondly, Nxt dreams must have some basis in reality. They must take into account your skills, strengths, attitude, and desires. Ideally, your Nxt dream will be an idea that inspires you to ask and answer a ton of questions—and gets your heart palpitating with excitement.

Of the dreams you have for the future, which gets you the most excited? Which inspires you to ask and answer a ton of questions?

_____

_____

_____

_____

_____

_____

When you close your eyes, and dream about the life you really want, what comes to mind? Describe it in as much detail as you can.

_____

_____

_____

_____

_____

_____

What dream have you been working toward? Is it yours, or someone else's?

_____

_____

_____

_____

_____

_____

3. Capitalize on What You Do Best

Another important component for choosing your Nxt dream is to capitalize on things you do best and thrive while doing them. Everybody has things they're really good at, but as simple humans, we tend to take them for granted because we think if we know how to do them, it's probably no big deal. But it is a big deal. It's time you came to terms with the fact that you have superpowers. Identify them, embrace them, and use them to make your Nxt dream come true.

List 3-6 things you do really well.

1. _____

_____

2. _____

_____

3. _____

_____

4. _____

_____

5. _____

_____

6. _____

_____

Which of the things you do really well would you describe as your superpowers?

_____

_____

_____

_____

_____

_____

_____

Which of your skills, strengths, and superpowers would you use more of if you could design the best way to work, the best kind of relationship, or the best lifestyle you could live?

Work:_____

_____

_____

_____

_____

_____

_____

_____

_____

_____

Relationship:_____

_____

_____

_____

_____

_____

_____

_____

_____

_____

_____

Lifestyle: _____

_____

_____

_____

_____

_____

_____

_____

_____

_____

_____

Notes, Thoughts, and Personal Musings

3

Break the Blockers

CHAPTER 3

Break the Blockers

I called a realtor I knew and told her about the (silly) dream I had about "retiring" on a beautiful piece of land with a gorgeous view, and how I thought I was ready to start looking at properties in the area. I also told her I was unsure about any other details to help narrow down the search.

After two days of touring properties, all I could talk about were each property's faults.

Clearly, I was blocked and shutting down everything about this dream before we even got started. All I could see were the *"buts"* and the *"what ifs,"* and they were keeping me from moving forward.

Lessons Learned

1. The Three Blockers of Change

How many times have you stopped yourself from moving into your Nxt because you have no idea what the future looks like, and that fear of the unknown is worse than staying where you are? Or how about those times you worried that if you did step forward, you might fail? Or maybe you believe it's easier to settle for what you have rather than exert the time and effort to try to make things better?

There are many reasons you can be blocked from moving into your Nxt, but I've found you can sum them up as the *Three Blockers of Change*. And they are:

- ⋄ Your Fear of the Unknown

- ⋄ Your Fear of Failure

- ⋄ Your Willingness to Settle

Each Blocker of Change is like a big red stop sign set up to keep you from seeing what could be. When you're blocked, it can feel like an insurmountable barrier. But experiencing any of these blockers is not an indication that you're uninterested in finding your Nxt. Any one of them can, however, paralyze you from making your next move.

Describe a situation when your Fear of the Unknown has stopped you from initiating a change in your work, your relationship, and your lifestyle.

Work: _____

_____

_____

_____

_____

_____

_____

_____

_____

_____

_____

Relationship:_____

_____

_____

_____

_____

_____

_____

_____

_____

_____

_____

Lifestyle: _____

_____

_____

_____

_____

_____

_____

_____

_____

_____

_____

_____

Describe a situation when your Fear of Failure has stopped you from initiating a change in your work, your relationship, and your lifestyle.

Work: _____

_____

_____

_____

_____

_____

_____

_____

_____

Relationship: _____

_____

_____

_____

_____

_____

_____

_____

_____

_____

Lifestyle: _____

_____

_____

_____

_____

_____

_____

_____

_____

_____

Describe a situation when your Willingness to Settle has stopped you from initiating a change in your work, your relationship, and your lifestyle.

Work: _____

_____

_____

_____

_____

_____

_____

_____

_____

Relationship:_____

_____

_____

_____

_____

_____

_____

_____

_____

_____

Lifestyle:_____

_____

_____

_____

_____

_____

_____

_____

_____

_____

2. Break Through the Blockers

Learning about the Blockers of Change, recognizing them, and seeing them for what they are will help you kick them out of the way so you can move toward finding your Nxt. Like it or not, you can't move into your Nxt dream or your Nxt stage in life until you learn how to identify and break through the blockers that are stopping you. Here are some tips.

A. First:, stop using "but . . . " and instead say "and . . . "

For example, it's blocking us from moving forward if we say: "I really need to look for a new job because my boss is a terrible person to work for, *but* I don't think I could find anything else that pays me what I earn here."

Or you could open up the possibilities for finding your Nxt by saying: "I really need to look for a new job because my boss is a terrible person to work for, *and* I'll have to search for a position that pays me what I'm earning here, *and* I'll need to make sure the person I'll be reporting to is a decent human being!"

What are 3 examples of things you have said when using the word "but"? Rewrite that same sentence, substituting the word "and" for the "but."

Example 1:

Using the word *"but"*: _____

_____

_____

_____

Now, replace the *"but"* with *"and"* in the same sentence: _____

_____

_____

_____

Example 2:

Using the word *"but"*: _____

_____

_____

_____

Now, replace the *"but"* with *"and"* in the same sentence: _____

_____

_____

_____

Example 3:

Using the word *"but"*: _____

_____

_____

_____

Now, replace the *"but"* with *"and"* in the same sentence: _____

_____

_____

_____

B. Stop looking for problems and start looking for solutions

The reality is, you don't know if a lot of things will work until you try them, and you don't have all the answers until you ask the questions and seek the information to fill in the blanks.

Often the power of a blocker is based on our need for more information. I mean, who wants to make a change from what we know to what we don't know, without having enough data to help us make a good decision?

What situation or dream have you been blocked from pursuing because you didn't have enough information to make a decision to move forward?

_____

_____

_____

_____

_____

What could you have done to gather more information to help you make a decision?

_____

_____

_____

_____

_____

C. Try playing the game "What's the Worst that Can Happen?"
A game you can play to help break through the blockers is to ask yourself "What's the worst that can happen?" if you choose to move forward with a given situation or opportunity.

For me, anything short of maiming or death means I can probably deal with any outcome if I choose to move forward. And, it usually takes me about 5 or 6 levels of "Then, what could happen?" before I hit that extreme level of consequence (if at all).

Typically, this exercise will demonstrate that *calling out* what you believe is the worst that can happen is often far less daunting and scary than your brain believes is the worst that can happen.

Name a situation (like "getting a new job" or "moving to a new town" or whatever you can think of that might cause you great fear of moving forward) and play the game, "What's the worst that can happen?" breaking it down to at least 4-6 levels.

Situation:_____

What's the Worst that Can Happen?

1. _____

Okay . . . if that happens, then what's the worst that can happen . . . .next?

2. _____

Okay . . . if that happens, then what's the worst that can happen . . . .next?

3. _____

Okay . . . if that happens, then what's the worst that can happen . . . .next?

4. _____

Okay . . . if that happens, then what's the worst that can happen . . . .next?

5. _____

Okay . . . if that happens, then what's the worst that can happen . . . .next?

6. _____

Notes, Thoughts, and Personal Musings

4

See What's Nxt

CHAPTER 4

See What's Nxt

Before starting our next real estate search, I made a list of everything I thought we'd like to find in a property and as luck would have it (timing had a lot to do with it), we found a piece of land that not only met the criteria on my list, but also took my breath away. It was the most beautiful, calming, majestic views I had ever seen. But it was also a much more dramatic Nxt level change than anything I had been considering until then.

The crazy thing was that I could see my dream unfolding before my eyes on that land. I couldn't see the exact house we would end up building, or where the garden would go, or the kinds of animals we'd have one day, but I could see the possibilities for building it all.

I could see the Nxt chapter of my life laid out before me. And it filled me up.

Lessons Learned

1. What Do You See?

In the early stages of finding your Nxt, it's important to define what you want your Nxt to do *for you*. At this point in the process, you probably won't be able to define the specifics of how you'll do it, but you can use your mind's eye to visualize the *big picture* of how your dream can play out in your future. You'll have plenty of time to dig into the details once you've had the chance to focus on your idea, so don't force yourself to dig in too deeply too quickly. Take your time. Watch your dream unfold before your eyes and imagine the possibilities of what *could be*.

What do you think the ideal version of your Nxt dream would look like?

_____

_____

_____

_____

_____

What do you want your Nxt step or stage in life to *do* for you?

_____

_____

_____

_____

_____

2. Sometimes You Have to Close your Eyes to See Clearly

When you close your eyes, you're not limited by what you already see. You can paint a picture of the possibilities you want to create and design for yourself. You can use broad strokes to illustrate what you want your dream to feel like and do for you, allowing yourself to describe an ideal scenario for how you want your Nxt to be, with no constraints. No blockers getting in your way. No details about how you'll do it. No limitations. Just a wide-open canvas on which you'll paint the big picture of what your Nxt step could do for you.

Close your eyes and imagine what could be Nxt for you. What do you see? Describe it.

_____

_____

_____

_____

_____

_____

_____

_____

_____

_____

_____

Imagine what "working" would look like if you could design it for yourself? Describe it.

_____

_____

_____

_____

_____

_____

_____

_____

Imagine what your ideal relationship would look like if you could design it for yourself?

Describe it.

_____

_____

_____

_____

_____

_____

_____

_____

Imagine what your ideal lifestyle would look like if you could design it for yourself?

Describe it.

_____

_____

_____

_____

_____

_____

_____

_____

_____

3. Be Open to the Evolution of Your Dream

Rarely is the first iteration of your dream the one you end up fully pursuing. It's amazing how many twists and turns your initial idea will take as you begin to search out the right path to finding your Nxt. As you gather more information, refine your thinking, and discover more opportunities as they present themselves, you'll often come to a place where your Nxt is a different version—most often a better version—of the original dream you thought you wanted.

Describe a time when you set out on one journey, only to find you ended up doing something that had evolved onto a different path.

_____

_____

_____

_____

_____

_____

What lessons did you learn from allowing yourself to evolve from your original dream to what actually happened?

_____

_____

_____

_____

_____

_____

Notes, Thoughts, and Personal Musings

5

Find Alignment

Find Alignment

Not long after we closed on the land, my mom Del decided it was time to go be with my dad Paul, who had passed away six years earlier. I had only recently purchased the property in Ridgway when my mom passed, but I had always known that both my mom and dad wanted their ashes spread together somewhere in Colorado, with their one caveat being that it had to be a place with gorgeous views. The more I thought about it, the more it became obvious that the Ridgway property would be their perfect resting place. But I still wasn't sure my idea was the right decision.

After my mom's memorial, our closest family members and friends took a drive down to the property to spread my parents ashes together under a couple of old cottonwoods we found on the property that we later dubbed "the grandparent trees." As our ad hoc ceremony came to a close, a double rainbow appeared in the sky, sending a signal to us all that Del and Paul were indeed in their perfect place. That sign made me realize what had been nagging at me: I hadn't felt aligned in my head, my heart and my gut about my decision.

Lessons Learned

1. Achieving Alignment

Confusion can easily set into decision-making when your rational thinking (your head), your purpose and values (your heart) and your built-in danger detector (your gut) aren't aligned.

Which of the three (head, heart or gut) do you tend to rely on most when making decisions?

_____

Which of the three (head, heart or gut) do you believe you need to listen to more? Why?

_____

_____

_____

_____

Describe a situation when you should have listened to your head, heart and gut when making a decision? Why?

_____

_____

_____

_____

_____

_____

_____

Describe a decision you've made when you've felt in total alignment between your head, heart and gut.

_____

_____

_____

_____

_____

_____

_____

2. Doubting Yourself

There might be times when figuring out what's Nxt that you doubt yourself and your ability to make the changes or decisions to move forward. It's natural and expected. If this happens, it's best to look at whether there are any missing pieces of information you need, in order to gain the confidence to move forward with your decision.

Pick a decision you might be having trouble making right now, and ask yourself the following questions:

Are your head, heart and gut all in alignment?_____

Do you have what you need to move forward? _____

Do your values align with what you are planning to do?_____

Is your gut sounding any alarms, or it is calm and quiet?_____

What is this all telling you? _____

Notes, Thoughts, and Personal Musings

6

Define What's Important

CHAPTER 6

Define What's Important

It was finally time to begin envisioning the kind of house that would be center stage for this Nxt stage of life. And yet, I had no idea how to build a house from the ground up. And it wasn't just the house. It was the whole place. The land. The location. The openness. The freedom. There were so many ways we could do this.

We realized this wasn't just a house we were building, but a whole new way of living. So we needed to take the time to focus on what was really important for us in designing our dream lifestyle. Which meant we needed to begin by defining our "Big Why."

Lessons Learned

1. Define Your Reasons for Why You're Making a Change

Knowing the reasons for making a change in your life will help you understand the importance of taking it to the next step. And here's the thing: if you're going to take the time and make the effort to step into your Nxt, don't you think you should be really clear on the reasons behind making that change in your life?

What are the overarching reasons for making a change in your life?

_____

_____

_____

_____

_____

_____

What will the benefits be if you make this change?

_____

_____

_____

_____

_____

_____

_____

2. What is Your Big Why?

Most businesses have mission statements to help align their workforce toward a common set of principles and purposes. In the same way, being able to articulate your own personal Big Why helps to clarify and align the practices and values by which you'll live your life. Regardless of whether your Nxt is about your lifestyle, your work, or your relationship, having clarity about what matters most to you is invaluable as you move through the process.

Our natural tendency is to begin with a more tactical approach when seeking something new. However, if you identify what is *most* important to you *first,* you'll gain a sense of certainty right out of the gate about what you'll need to have in order to succeed, be happy, and be fulfilled in your Nxt.

List out what you believe are the 6 *most* important elements to be included in your Nxt.

1. _____

   _____

   _____

2. _____

   _____

   _____

3. _____

   _____

   _____

4. _____

   _____

   _____

5. _____

   _____

   _____

6. _____

   _____

   _____

What's most important to you in order to thrive when *working?* List out words or phrases that come to you without self-editing.

_____   _____   _____

_____   _____   _____

_____   _____   _____

_____   _____   _____

_____   _____   _____

_____   _____   _____

What do you need in order to thrive in your *primary relationship?* List out words or phrases that come to you without self-editing.

_____   _____   _____

_____   _____   _____

_____   _____   _____

_____   _____   _____

_____   _____   _____

_____   _____   _____

What would be the most important components to have, or do, in order to design the *lifestyle you want to live?* List out words or phrases that come to you without self-editing.

_____   _____   _____

_____   _____   _____

_____   _____   _____

_____   _____   _____

_____   _____   _____

_____   _____   _____

Now, Pick out the 4-6 MOST IMPORTANT things *about working* (from your list above) that would be deal breakers for you if you didn't have them.

1. _____

2. _____

3. _____

4. _____

5. _____

6. _____

Pick out the 4-6 MOST IMPORTANT things you really need from your *primary relationship* (from your list above) that would be deal breakers for you if you didn't have them.

1. _____

2. _____

3. _____

4. _____

5. _____

6. _____

Pick out the 4-6 MOST IMPORTANT things about the *lifestyle you really want to live* (from your list above) that you wouldn't want to live without.

1. _____

2. _____

3. _____

4. _____

5. _____

6. _____

3. Hard Yes, Easy No

Most of us have an easier time saying yes than no. We tend to want to be accommodating and nice and thoughtful, and it can feel hard to say no. Often, we will push aside whatever might be important to us in favor of a request from someone else, because we don't want to let them down or put them in a bind or because it feels good to help.

Having a list of what is most important to you—and holding it sacred—is the only way to move from the *Easy Yes/Hard No* to the *Hard Yes/Easy No*. I'm not talking about becoming a selfish, rude, or bitchy person who, because you know what's important to you, totally negates what's important to someone else. I'm talking about recognizing that what's *most important to you* should have tremendous weight when making important decisions that will lead to your Nxt.

Finding your Nxt should meet as many of the criteria of what's most important to you as possible, so you can use your list as criteria for making decisions!

Using your list of the 4-6 most important things that allow you to thrive when working, describe how they apply, or do not apply, to your **current way of working.**

_____

_____

_____

_____

_____

_____

What could you do to ensure that all of the things most important to you can show up?

_____

_____

_____

_____

Using your list of the 4-6 most important things that you need in your primary relationship, describe how they apply, or do not apply, to your *current primary relationship.*

_____

_____

_____

_____

_____

What could you do to ensure that all of the things most important to you can show up?

_____

_____

_____

_____

Using your list of the 4-6 most important components that you want to include in the lifestyle you want to live, describe how they apply, or do not apply, to your *current lifestyle.*

_____

_____

_____

_____

_____

What could you do to ensure that all of the things most important to you can show up?

_____

_____

_____

_____

4. Can I say Yes Without Checking All the Boxes?

If you choose to move forward with a Nxt step that doesn't check all of your criteria boxes, then do so intentionally. That's OK. There are certainly times when circumstances dictate that it is more prudent to start with a partial list checked off and work toward adding the other important concepts down the road, but it must be an intentional decision.

List out different circumstances that might compel you to intentionally move forward without one (or more) of your boxes being checked:

When working

_____

_____

_____

_____

In your Primary Relationship

_____

_____

_____

_____

With your Lifestyle

_____

_____

_____

_____

Notes, Thoughts, and Personal Musings

7

Naming CC Blue

CHAPTER 7

Naming CC Blue

This is the chapter describing the process of naming our Ranch . . . CC Blue.

Lessons Learned

There really aren't any major lessons here, other than to think about the importance behind a name. For a person, a piece of land, or a business, names are important.

Notes, Thoughts, and Personal Musings

_____
_____
_____
_____
_____
_____
_____
_____
_____
_____
_____
_____
_____
_____
_____
_____
_____
_____
_____
_____
_____
_____
_____

8

Live with Intention

CHAPTER 8

Live with Intention

As I began to dream about the idea of finding a beautiful piece of property in the mountains with a gorgeous view, Matthew was the one I shared it all with. He was a part of the process from that first trip to look at properties to defining what was most important about creating CC Blue.

At no time during that whole process, however, did we sit down and have a serious conversation about what we each wanted in terms of our relationship, both on and off the Ranch. It felt like we were being swept up in the momentum of it all, and we'd never made a conscious choice to do this Nxt together. We were just going with the flow, and our lives started to feel directionless.

We had hit that point in the process of Finding this Nxt when we needed to have more definition and structure about what we were doing together. It was time to stop momentum from taking us down the stream and intentionally put our oars in the water and steer in a direction we chose. In other words, it was time to make a commitment to what we wanted this Nxt *to be*.

Lessons Learned

1. Be Intentional

You can move in a direction intentionally, or you can let momentum take you down the path of least resistance. Intentionality is about deciding to move in one direction versus another, or to do one thing or another, consciously choosing between options. As you find and move into your Nxt, you'll (of course) want to think through all the possibilities, all the different scenarios, and play out all the pros and cons in your mind.

Are you experiencing momentum in moving you forward without intentionality? Describe it.

_____

_____

_____

_____

Describe your Nxt opportunity or dream and list out the pros and cons for moving forward.

Pros	Cons
_____	_____
_____	_____
_____	_____
_____	_____
_____	_____
_____	_____

What's missing from being able to make a commitment to move forward?

_____

_____

_____

What might be blocking you from making a commitment to move forward?

_____

_____

_____

_____

_____

Are you ready to make a commitment to step into your Nxt?

_____ YES!

_____ No, I still need to figure some things out (as I recognize now from answering the questions above)

2. Harness the Power of Momentum

Momentum equals movement, which you can initiate to create the energy to move you forward, or momentum can be instigated by the circumstances around you, forcing you to move in a direction you may or may not want to go. Regardless of the way it's created, there is an energy that comes with momentum. The trick is to consciously create momentum and use it to move you where you want to go, rather than put yourself in a situation where momentum happens to you.

What are 3-5 ways in which you could consciously create momentum to move you forward in the ***work you do?***

1. _____

_____

2. _____

_____

3. _____

_____

4. _____

_____

5. _____

_____

What are 3-5 ways in which you could consciously create momentum to move you forward in your ***primary relationship?***

1. _____

_____

2. _____

_____

3. _____

_____

4. _____

_____

5. _____

_____

What are 3-5 ways in which you could consciously create momentum to move you forward in creating the *lifestyle you want to live?*

1. _____

_____

2. _____

_____

3. _____

_____

4. _____

_____

5. _____

_____

3. Put a Stake in the Ground

Here's the deal: A life change (i.e., Your Nxt) doesn't *probably* happen. It happens when you make a declaration that you're going to make it happen. You have to put a stake in the ground and declare that you are going to do it. Whatever it is.

Declare your Nxt! What is it?

Date _____   Signature _____ (now it's real!)

_____

_____

_____

_____

_____

_____

Notes, Thoughts, and Personal Musings

_____
_____
_____
_____
_____
_____
_____
_____
_____
_____
_____
_____
_____
_____
_____
_____
_____
_____
_____
_____
_____
_____
_____
_____

9

Bring Your Life with You

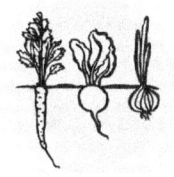

CHAPTER 9

Bring Your Life with You

When I bought the property, I may or may not have romantically imagined myself homesteading like they did on the TV show *Little House on the Prairie* (but with a much nicer house and a lot more modern conveniences than they ever imagined). I don't know exactly what I thought I was stepping into, but I do know it didn't include any thoughts about what life on a ranch *really* meant, and I certain didn't consider myself to be *homesteading*.

What I did imagine life on the Ranch including was the creation of a self-sufficient lifestyle. But I'm not sure I had any idea what that meant. Nor did I believe at the start of the adventure that I would be able to figure it out. But I was selling myself short.

I got to bring with me everything I had learned and experienced in my life before CC Blue. I had a wealth of knowledge and experience that provided me with many of the qualities, skills, and strengths I would need to build this Nxt life. Everything from my organizational and business skills to my design, decorating, and entertaining expertise.

Lessons Learned

1. Life Builds upon Itself

When your Nxt is something you've never done before, it's easy to disregard everything you've done in the past because what's in front of you is so different. However, you actually get to take everything you've done in your past life with you and apply it to your Nxt.

That's right! You get to use everything you've ever learned in the past and build upon it as you move into your Nxt!

List out all of the different jobs you've had in your life and the skills that you developed while doing that job.

Job: _____

Skills you either learned or used on the job:

_____

_____

_____

_____

_____

Job: _____

Skills you either learned or used on the job:

_____

_____

_____

_____

_____

Job: _____

Skills you either learned or used on the job:

_____

_____

_____

_____

_____

Job: _____

Skills you either learned or used on the job:

_____

_____

_____

_____

_____

Job: _____

Skills you either learned or used on the job:

_____

_____

_____

_____

_____

2. Your Skills Come with You

Skill: The Ability to Do Something Well

Summarize all of your skills (from the preceding lists) that will come with you into your Nxt:

1. _____

2. _____

3. _____

4. _____

5. _____

6. _____

7. _____

8. _____

9. _____

10. _____

11. _____

12. _____

13. _____

14. _____

15. _____

16. _____

17. _____

18. _____

19. _____

20. _____

21. _____

22. _____

23. _____

24. _____

25. _____

3. Identify and Capitalize on Your Strengths

Strengths—Character Traits that are Positive

Starting from a place of strength is especially important when stepping into something new. Knowing whether you're a strong leader or a wonderful independent thinker; whether you thrive with data and information before deciding or you'd rather get input from others before taking action; whether you're a strategic thinker or more of a real-time doer (just to name a few strengths) will help you understand what you can leverage from within, and how you can thrive in your Nxt.

What are all of your strengths (don't hold back—list them all!) that you get to bring with you into your Nxt?

1. _____
2. _____
3. _____
4. _____
5. _____
6. _____
7. _____
8. _____
9. _____
10. _____
11. _____
12. _____
13. _____
14. _____
15. _____
16. _____
17. _____
18. _____
19. _____
20. _____

Notes, Thoughts, and Personal Musings

10

Figure it Out

CHAPTER 10

Figure it Out

The idea of homesteading expanded dramatically with the introduction of our first animals—chickens—onto the farm. At first it seemed like an easy decision to bring chickens onto the property, but it took a lot of trial and error to learn how to raise them.

We had to think through what kind of chickens to get and then be prepared with the proper setup once they arrived. We had to be thoughtful about their shelter and safety and learn what they would need to thrive as they grew into adulthood. We had to educate ourselves and accept responsibility for their well-being. By doing so, we finally received the benefit of having beautiful, healthy chickens with delicious blue farm-fresh eggs for ourselves.

Lessons Learned

1. Take Your Decisions Seriously

Even if your Nxt doesn't have life and death consequences associated with it, the decisions at every step of the way should always be taken seriously. It could mean a major change in your life. It could affect your income, your relationship, or your way of living. There are always consequences for our behaviors and actions, and even if we are not solely responsible for each repercussion, we should act as if we are.

What are some consequences or repercussions of stepping into your Nxt that you should keep at the forefront of your mind when evaluating next actions?

1._____

2._____

3._____

4. _____

5._____

6._____

2. Take Your Decisions Seriously

Starting Your Nxt journey may not work out as planned the first time, and that's OK. Trial and error forces you to understand what's wrong with your initial assumptions, what's missing from your information, and what you didn't know when you started out. The important thing is to adapt, adjust, and redesign plans to reflect your increased knowledge before moving forward again.

What has already changed from your initial plan for your Nxt?

_____

_____

_____

_____

What assumptions did you make that you now understand were in error?

_____

_____

_____

_____

What pieces of information were missing that you have now learned?

_____

_____

_____

_____

_____

What adaptions, adjustments, or redesigns of your initial plan have you made?

_____

_____

_____

_____

_____

3. Learn from Your Mistakes

When Finding Your Nxt, learning from your mistakes is crucial to moving forward. There's no such thing as failure when moving into your Nxt, just gaining more information and insight, as long as you are willing to learn and adjust accordingly.

Our mistakes on the Ranch are almost too numerous to count. But we learned and grew. We adapted our behaviors and redesigned the way we did things. Every lesson has made things better.

What lessons have you learned from moving toward your Nxt so far?

_____

_____

_____

_____

_____

In what ways have you adapted your behaviors to meet the needs you have identified?

_____

_____

_____

_____

_____

How have you redesigned the plan for your Nxt in relation to what you have learned so far?

_____

_____

_____

_____

_____

_____

_____

_____

_____

_____

Notes, Thoughts, and Personal Musings

II

---

*Determine
Your Criteria*

CHAPTER 11

Determine Your Criteria

Now that we had successfully incorporated chickens into our lifestyle, I turned my attention to adding more animals on the Ranch. There was a large herd of beautiful black-and-white cows on our neighbors' property, and I would watch them grazing from my office. I was enamored by how they enhanced the view. They were a Scottish breed called "Belted Galloways" and they were beautiful! They weren't an ordinary-looking cow (which I liked), more like a large Oreo cookie with black furry coats and a broad white band wrapped around their mid-sections—and I thought they'd make a perfect addition to CC Blue.

Of course, we knew nothing about raising cows, but like everything else, we would figure it out.

Lessons Learned

1. Determine Your Criteria (Breaking Down Your "Big Why.")
Criteria: a principle or standard by which something may be judged or decided.

Sometimes when we think about what's Nxt, we assume it will be *one* thing. One change. One decision. One addition of something to our lives. Or one next step to get there. In reality, sometimes there can be *multiple next steps* to finding, and *achieving*, your Nxt.

Once you have an overarching theme for what you are trying to accomplish, determining the criteria for each step of your Nxt creates the context for you to work within. This allows you to narrow the specific actions needed to make it happen.

Determining your criteria *before* you take any action, also helps you define specific tasks necessary to achieving your goals. These tasks might include a list of work requirements, people requirements, or even value adjustments.

Begin with a broad stroke of what you want your Nxt to accomplish for you, and then break down the criteria for your actions, followed by the specific tasks required for success.

Once again, what do you want your Nxt to accomplish for you? (Has it become more focused we first started?)

_____

_____

_____

_____

_____

_____

_____

What are the criteria at each step?

An example for us to bring cows onto the property was:

Step One: _Install Fencing for the Cows_

    Criteria for action: 1) _The fencing needs to go around the entire perimeter of the pasture_

                      2) _It needs to be strong enough to hold the cows inside the pasture_

                      3) _It needs to be high enough so the cows can't jump over it_

Now list *your* steps and criteria.

Step One: _____

    Criteria for action: 1) _____

                           2) _____

                           3) _____

Step Two: _____

    Criteria for action: 1) _____

                           2) _____

                           3) _____

Step Three: _____

    Criteria for action: 1) _____

                           2) _____

                           3) _____

What are the specific tasks necessary for each action to be successful?

An example for us to get the fencing done was:

Action: Install the Fencing _____

          Task: Research local fencing companies and get bids ____

          Task: Schedule fencing company to do the work _____

Now list *your* actions and tasks.

Action: _____

          Task: _____

          Task: _____

Action: _____

      Task: _____

      Task: _____

Action: _____

      Task: _____

      Task: _____

Action: _____

      Task: _____

      Task: _____

2. Understand the Benefits

Benefit: an advantage or profit gained from something.

Understanding the benefits behind your actions helps ensure you continue to relate your decisions to what is most important to you. It can be easy to get caught up in the more tactical exercises of setting up the criteria for your actions and forget to identify and acknowledge the benefits of doing so.

List out the top 5 benefits you will realize once you accomplish your Nxt.

1. _____

2. _____

3. _____

4. _____

5. _____

What are the 3 most important benefits from each of the steps (from earlier in this section)?

Step One: _____

      Benefit: _____

      Benefit: _____

      Benefit: _____

Step Two: _____

      Benefit: _____

      Benefit: _____

      Benefit: _____

Step Three: _____

      Benefit: _____

      Benefit: _____

      Benefit: _____

Step Four: _____

      Benefit: _____

      Benefit: _____

      Benefit: _____

Step Five: _____

      Benefit: _____

      Benefit: _____

      Benefit: _____

Notes, Thoughts, and Personal Musings

12

Make It Up

CHAPTER 12

Make It Up

After we felt like we had a handle on raising cows, our dream of raising more farm animals started to become a frequent topic of conversation. It may not make sense, but the idea of adding more animals into our lives felt like an even bigger decision than pulling the trigger to move to the Ranch in the first place. It was a lot more responsibility, but the bigger issue was that I was hung up on the idea that there was a particular way we were *supposed* to do it. And, as always, I wanted to make it up and do it *our own way*.

The challenge was, as much as I wanted to make up the way to do it, we were dealing with real live animals. I was worried there was some magic formula we needed to follow for running a farm in a particular way, with a particular configuration of animals. I figured there had to be a blueprint, or at the very least, rules about doing the whole farm animal thing, *right*?

Well, there wasn't.

Lessons Learned

1. Making It Up Requires a Different Perspective (It's time to get creative!)

Sometimes we need to release ourselves from the belief that there is only one way to do things. Further, we don't need to be locked into the way something is supposed to be done just because someone has done it a certain way before us. The idea of making it up is a way of challenging yourself to think differently about how to look at a problem or an opportunity. Instead of assuming there is a required way to get a problem solved, you can ask yourself: *How man different ideas can I brainstorm that will still meet my needs?*

Try to list 5-10 different ways than it's ever been done before—which one that serves you far better than you ever thought possible before?

Based on your developing idea of your Nxt, what are some new things you can experiment with to best meet your needs?

_____

_____

_____

_____

_____

_____

_____

_____

_____

_____

_____

_____

_____

2. We've Always Done It That Way

We often feel stuck because we're in a loop of feeling like the way we've always done something is the way it *has to be done*, simply because we've always done it that way. Our perspective about a problem or solution often begins from a place of *what it is*, rather than the ideal situation of what it *could be* to meet our needs.

Taking into account your *Big Why*, and the *criteria* you laid out earlier, what are some things you're presently doing you feel aren't working for you now? What might be some better approaches?

_____

_____

_____

_____

_____

_____

_____

_____

_____

_____

_____

3. Intention Versus Momentum (Revisited because it's that important)

Remember from Chapter Eight: Deciding to act meant you were moving forward with *intention*, not simply being *swept along by momentum*.

Here, we are talking about using momentum as a *positive tool* to take hold of the change process once you get the ball rolling. Once you know the direction you are going in, and what you are working toward, you can *create momentum* to move you forward and keep your energy flowing along the way!

How are you using momentum as a positive tool to move you forward?

_____

_____

_____

_____

_____

_____

What are some action steps you can initiate to create momentum for yourself to help move you forward into your Nxt?

_____

_____

_____

_____

_____

_____

_____

_____

_____

_____

_____

Notes, Thoughts, and Personal Musings

ß

Step Into Your Nxt

CHAPTER 13

Step Into Your Nxt

Not long after the barn was full of animals and we felt pretty darn settled into our new life, I decided it was time to step it up even more by birthing some animal babies on the Ranch. A voice inside me kept saying that until we bred our own animals, we weren't real ranchers. And I wanted to be a *real* ranch girl.

So, after some discussion, we decided to begin with breeding our goats, because I knew baby goats would increase the cuteness quotient on the Ranch tenfold, and you know that "cuteness" always factored into my decision-making with our animals.

This was the time for me to step into my Nxt, and little did I know all that would entail. Things were about to get very real.

Lessons Learned

1. Playing a Role

It's perfectly natural to feel awkward or unsure and a bit like an imposter when you enter into a Nxt phase of your life. Especially if it's super different from anything you've done before. But even if you're making a small adjustment to your career, relationship, or your lifestyle, you can still feel like you're faking it or playing a role until something happens that convinces you that you belong where you are. It's the nature of change.

In what way(s) do you feel like an imposter, or that you're playing a role in your Nxt?

_____

_____

_____

_____

_____

_____

_____

What do you think you'll need to experience, or learn for yourself, before you are fully able to step into your Nxt?

_____

_____

_____

_____

_____

_____

_____

_____

_____

_____

_____

2. Identifying with Your Nxt Self

Many of us share a fear of having to choose between our current and our Nxt identity—believing we have to *give up* the former to get to the latter. The thing is you don't have to give up anything. You don't have to *choose* between one identity and a Nxt one. Your Nxt self will always encompass all of the parts of you—your experience, your knowledge, and your achievements (and your past titles)—when you allow those things to blend into your expanded Nxt self. In other words, you get to *add new* (bonus!) stuff onto who you've already been. (And who you already are!)

Make a list of everything you believe is wrapped up in your current identity, and then add to it what new (bonus!) stuff your Nxt will provide for you:

Current Identity	Added (Bonus!) Stuff from Your Nxt
_____	_____
_____	_____
_____	_____
_____	_____
_____	_____
_____	_____
_____	_____

Notes, Thoughts, and Personal Musings

14

Know Your Number

CHAPTER 14

Know Your Number

The first few years of living on the Ranch were all about building the infrastructure which, quite frankly, meant a lot more money was going *out* the door than was coming back *in*. So it was time to think about earning again. The challenge was to create the *right kind of business* to fit our lifestyle and we knew we didn't have enough acreage to earn a living entirely through ranching or farming.

As luck would have it, we heard there was a shortage of hotel rooms in the area, so we decided to go into the "short-term rental" business and put our Guest House on Airbnb, which ended up being a great business for us to run on the property, but also required a ton of time and work. We had no problem doing what was necessary to run the business, but we weren't sure we could justify all of the effort it took to earn enough money to live the life we wanted.

The problem: We had no idea what *enough money* actually meant in terms of an actual *number*.

Lessons Learned

1. Do the Math

When I was the CEO of my company, I ran it with the following philosophy: "I like big numbers and I like adding to them. So let's run this business without subtracting."

It was a ridiculous statement to make and typically made everyone laugh, but it also put everyone into a mindset of growth. So we decided to run the business on the Ranch the same way.

To begin, we needed to add up all of the *costs* associated with our life on the Ranch. Otherwise, we were making decisions about our business by making assumptions about what it cost us to run things—rather than making decisions from data (i.e. the real numbers).

To know your numbers, you must be willing to gather all of the information and do the math.

What are the *monthly* costs (expenses) for running your life?
(Expense categories for a business are different)

Mortgage or Rent: $ _____

Automobile Payments: $ _____

Utilities: $ _____

Technology costs (phones/cable/streaming/internet) $ _____

Insurance (home/renters, auto, health) $ _____

Gas $ _____

Food $ _____

Personal Services $ _____

Entertainment $ _____

Travel $ _____

Contribution to Savings $ _____

Contribution to 401(k)/Investments $ _____

Miscellaneous $ _____

Total Monthly Expenses $ _____

This is your Break-even Number—the number that tells you what you *need to earn* to meet your expenses. It's your bottom-line. It defines the amount of income you have to earn in order to maintain the life you currently live. It's a crucial number for you to know.

What is the *monthly* income you currently have (from all sources)?
(Income/revenue sources will be different for a business)

From your job(s) $ _____

Rental income $ _____

Child Support/Marital Support $ _____

Investment income $ _____

Other _____ $ _____

Total Monthly Income $ _____

Next, subtract your total monthly expenses from your total monthly income:

Total Monthly Income $ _____

Total Monthly Expense $ – _____

What's Left Over $ _____

If you are earning just enough to cover your expenses, you are living a Break-even life. If you are earning more than you are spending, then you are living with some Profit.

Now the question is, what are you working toward?

2. What Are You Working Toward

Once you know what your current finances are, you can begin to explore what new Break-even or Profit Number you'll need to strive for, in order to live the Nxt stage of your life, and what additional resources (money, time, etc.) you will need to do so. Maybe you'd like to go on a trip to Italy or purchase a better car. Or maybe you'd like to be able to take that raft trip through the Grand Canyon. It doesn't matter *what it is*. What matters is that you allow yourself to dream about what you want to *add* into your life in order to grow into your ideal Nxt. Then you can plan to get there.

What would you want to include in your life that you don't have now?

1. _____

2. _____

3. _____

4. _____

5. _____

6. _____

Describe how your life would look if you could include what you listed above?

_____

_____

_____

_____

_____

_____

You might have to do a little research to answer this next question, but what would it cost you to do each of the things you listed above? *Please don't assume you can't afford it, so why bother figuring out the costs. This exercise is designed to provide you with important (and real) information so you know the numbers and can make a plan to earn and achieve the life you want.*

_____	$_____
_____	$_____
_____	$_____
_____	$_____
_____	$_____
_____	$_____
_____	$_____
_____	$_____
_____	$_____
_____	$_____

3. Have a Profit Mentality

Profitability is not a new concept, but it's an idea that has been assigned almost entirely to running a business, not to our personal lives. Successful business owners don't operate with a break-even mentality. They operate with a profit mentality. They grow and invest in their company and their people. When you have a personal profit mentality, you operate your life expecting you will invest in yourself (and your family) and your lifestyle. You do this by making decisions about ways in which you can earn *more than* your Break-even Number to live the life you want.

This requires that you declare a number that you are working toward—that will give you the financial resources to live the life you want to live.

What is the Number you are working toward? $_____

4. Make it a Game

Money is a big issue when finding your Nxt. So we have to deal with it. Otherwise the process of finding your Nxt is all theoretical, and you won't be able to turn your ideas into an actionable plan. If you've come this far in the process, it's worth your time to get practical and tactical. Dealing with the money part of your Nxt is essential to moving forward.

That doesn't mean it has to be dry and mathematical and, dare I say, all about creating a budget which can feel restrictive and cumbersome and boring. Instead, play the Break-even/Profit Number game!

First, create a twelve-month spreadsheet (your game board) at the start of every year.

A. Include all of your expenses in categories (mortgage/rent; utilities, etc.) down the left column and all twelve months of the year across the top, with a "total" column at the end. If any of your expenses are known and consistent, go ahead and fill in as much of the game board as you can.

B. On a lower section of the spreadsheet, list all of your income sources. If any are known and consistent, go ahead and fill in as much of the game board as you can.

C. Next, create a line at the bottom of the spreadsheet for your Profit Number. (*As part of my game, I like to spread my Profit Number evenly across the twelve months, because I like to try to earn a share of my annual Profit Number every month. I find it's more fun to take the "win" every month I hit my number*).

	JAN	FEB	MAR	APR	MAY	JUN	JUL	AUG	SEP	OCT	NOV	DEC	TOTAL
INCOME #1													
INCOME #2													
INCOME #3													
TOTAL INCOME													
EXPENSE #1													
EXPENSE #2													
EXPENSE #3													
EXPENSE #4													
TOTAL EXPENSE													
PROFIT NUMBER													

5. Play the Game

To "play" the game, track your numbers every month. It may sound time consuming, but it lets you play your game much more efficiently and in real time, allowing you to create more "wins" and choices for how you play the game along the way.

A. If you want to know whether or not you can afford to take a trip to Italy for example, "game it out" by plugging in the costs for the trip into your game board spreadsheet to see how all of the expenses affect both your Break-even and Profit Numbers.

You can see how it would look if you bought your airline tickets early in the year and paid them off over the next several months or paid for them in full in one month. You could do the same with your accommodations and saving up the money to take on the trip for food and fun.

B. Move the numbers around and adjust the timing to meet your needs . . . and in this way, you get to play the game to live the life you want!

Notes, Thoughts, and Personal Musings

15

Put it On the Calendar

CHAPTER 15

Put it On the Calendar

Now that we were in full swing with our animals and Airbnb business, it began to feel like all of our time was being taken up by the needs of the Ranch. As intentional as we were about bringing animals onto the property and turning our guest accommodations into a money-making machine, we didn't factor in both the commitment and how much *time* it all would require.

We stopped going out for dinner or making plans with friends. We weren't going on vacations. So what was going on with us? Why were we allowing ourselves to become tied to the life we had wanted to create?

The solution: We had to manage our time better, schedule differently, and prioritize more *intentionally*. (There's that word again!)

We started with the way we managed our calendar.

Lessons Learned

1. Set Your Priorities

If you really want to do something, you have to set your priorities and put them on the calendar.

Name three to five priorities for your life (examples: exercise, spend time with _____, write my book) that you haven't put on your calendar yet.

1._____

2._____

3._____

4._____

5._____

List out how often you want to do those priorities (i.e. every week; monthly or over the course of a year, etc.).

1._____ How often? _____

2._____ How often? _____

3._____ How often? _____

4._____ How often? _____

5._____ How often? _____

2. Make a Commitment

Putting your priorities into your calendar is the act of committing to do something. It's you deciding what you are going *to do*.

Place your priorities in your calendar, recognizing that this is your commitment to doing them.

3. Now Do It

Sometimes it feels risky and scary when you set a time frame to finally *do your Nxt*. But declaring *when* you will begin your Nxt allows you to work backward within the assigned time frame and create a plan.

What is the time frame to accomplish your Nxt?

Start date: _____

End date: _____

Working backwards from your end date to your start date, what are the steps and benchmarks you'll need to do?

Step 1 _____ Dates _____

Step 2 _____ Dates _____

Step 3 _____ Dates _____

Step 4 _____ Dates _____

Step 5 _____ Dates _____

Step 6 _____ Dates _____

Benchmark _____

Step 1 _____ Dates _____

Step 2 _____ Dates _____

Step 3 _____ Dates _____

Step 4 _____ Dates _____

Step 5 _____ Dates _____

Step 6 _____ Dates _____

Benchmark _____

Step 1 _____ Dates _____

Step 2 _____ Dates _____

Step 3 _____ Dates _____

Step 4 _____ Dates _____

Step 5 _____ Dates _____

Step 6 _____ Dates _____

Benchmark _____

Step 1 _____ Dates _____

Step 2 _____ Dates _____

Step 3 _____ Dates _____

Step 4 _____ Dates _____

Step 5 _____ Dates _____

Step 6 _____ Dates _____

Benchmark _____

Step 1 _____ Dates _____

Step 2 _____ Dates _____

Step 3 _____ Dates _____

Step 4 _____ Dates _____

Step 5 _____ Dates _____

Step 6 _____ Dates _____

Benchmark _____

Notes, Thoughts, and Personal Musings

.

16

---

*Create the
Perfect Blend*

CHAPTER 16

Create the Perfect Blend

From the start of finding my Nxt, I sought to create the perfect blend of my lifestyle, my relationship, and my work—to create the ideal life that I wanted to live. As I delved further into the question of how I wanted to work, I discovered that I could blend my love of business with my strengths and skills for mentoring, to create a new career path for myself—and started a coaching business.

As the vision expanded, I developed a whole new kind of coaching program that Matthew and I collaborate on together to provide an immersive experience at the Ranch—clients come here for two and half days—and we pamper them (Matthew does all of the hosting and cooking) while I do all of the coaching to help individuals, couples, and business partners find their Nxt.

It has turned out to be the perfect blend for us.

Lessons Learned

1. From Balance to Blend

Think about all the different parts of your life as *ingredients* that you get to blend together to create an amazing stew—with life being the pot.

What are the *major ingredients* of your life that form the foundation of your life's stew?

Ingredient: _____

Ingredient: _____

Ingredient: _____

Ingredient: _____

Ingredient: _____

Ingredient: _____

What are the ingredients that add *spice and flavor* to your life's stew? (Examples might be your work, family, children, sports, etc.)

Ingredient: _____

Ingredient: _____

Ingredient: _____

Ingredient: _____

Ingredient: _____

Ingredient: _____

2. Blending the Ingredients of Life

Describe the most ideal blend of a life you can imagine.

_____

_____

_____

_____

_____

_____

_____

What would you add to your current blend of life to attain the ideal blend you described above?

_____

_____

_____

_____

_____

_____

_____

How would you go about adding those things into your life to attain your Nxt life blend?

_____

_____

_____

_____

_____

_____

_____

_____

_____

_____

_____

Notes, Thoughts, and Personal Musings

Nxt Cheat Sheet

There are going to be many Nxt's—Nxt steps, Nxt phases and Nxt chapters—that you go through in your life. So. . . here's a cheat sheet with 5 of the MOST important questions to ask yourself whenever you find yourself moving toward your Nxt.

1. What is your Nxt Dream?

_____

_____

_____

_____

_____

_____

_____

_____

2. What is your *Big Why*?
(What is most important to you at this point in your life?)

_____

_____

_____

_____

_____

_____

_____

_____

3. What are you moving *toward* (intentionally)?

_____

_____

_____

_____

_____

_____

_____

_____

_____

_____

4. What's your (*new*) Number?
(And what's the difference from where you are now?)

_____

_____

_____

5. What is your timeframe for moving into your Nxt?
(Have you put it on the Calendar?)

_____

_____

_____

_____

_____

_____

_____

_____

_____

CONGRATULATIONS

on Finding Your Nxt!

I hope you found this Workbook to be helpful and thought provoking. I'm sure you didn't answer *every* question for all of the concepts, steps, and lessons for finding your Nxt, as not every one of them will apply to each Nxt you are going through.. But you might want to revisit the questions and exercises every now and then to refamiliarize yourself with what is most important to you for each new Nxt; any new criteria you need for decision-making; and to update your Number as you move through life.

If you get stuck and can't move through the process without some help, please feel free to reach out to me for some one-on-one coaching. I work with clients all over the world who need an objective perspective from someone they know has their best interest in mind. And if you don't want to reach out to me directly for help, please reach out to any of the zillions of coaches around the world to find someone you can talk with and trust.

If you're looking for a unique and personalized experience to figure out what's Nxt, please consider my Immersion program at CC Blue Ranch. I work directly with individuals, couples, or business partners, who come to the Ranch to be pampered and coached in person, in a safe and productive manner to help them gain clarity and define their path to move forward into their Nxt. No groups—just you alone, you and your spouse, or you and your business partner. It's a totally unique and individualized experience.

Thank you for taking the time to work through your Nxt step, chapter, or phase in life with this Workbook!

For more information about individual ongoing coaching or the
Immersion to Find Your Nxt program at CC Blue Ranch:

WEBSITE:
FindingYourNXT.com

EMAIL:
CindyKramCarrillo@gmail.com

INSTAGRAM:
@ccblueridgway

LINKEDIN:
Cindy (Kram) Carrillo

One-on-One

The Immersion

A multi-day, intensive deep dive into your life, career, and aspirations. Your Immersion program is tailored to you from start to finish. We focus on the areas that matter to you most and impact your success and happiness.

Nxt Coaching

For those seeking personal and professional growth at any stage of your career or life, Nxt Coaching provides tailored, one-on-one coaching to help you get where you want to go with confidance.

Visit the Finding Your Nxt website when you are ready to step into the life you really want.

findingyournxt.com

www.ingramcontent.com/pod-product-compliance
Lightning Source LLC
Chambersburg PA
CBHW082147120626
46553CB00010B/2805